SHORTHAND SYSTEMS OF THE WORLD

From the Memorial Portrait by A. Cope

SIR ISAAC PITMAN

Dr. John Robert Gregg

SHORTHAND SYSTEMS OF THE WORLD

A Concise Historical and Technical Review

H. GLATTE, A.B.S.C.

THE WISDOM LIBRARY

A Division of
PHILOSOPHICAL LIBRARY
New York

Copyright, 1959, by
Philosophical Library, Inc.
15 East 40th Street, New York

All rights reserved

Dedicated to

Gregor Hartmann

Set at the Polyglot Press, New York
Printed in the United States of America

CONTENTS

	Page
Introduction	7
Chapter	
I Development of Handwriting	9
II Ancient Shorthand	12
III Old British Geometrical Systems	16
IV British Influence Abroad	23
V Growth of the Cursive Systems	27
VI Modern British Geometrical Methods	33
VII Perfecting the Cursive Methods	39
VIII "Shorthand" Machines and Dictating Machines	55
Conclusion	59
Bibliography	63

Introduction

Handwriting is an art, and shorthand the perfection of that art.

In offering this little book I wish to widen interest in shorthand, encourage the perfection of an ideal system and remind those who have much writing to do of the great advantages of knowing shorthand oneself.

I would take this opportunity of thanking especially the following for the latest essential facts:

The Rev. J. Williams, M.A., of the British & Foreign Bible Society, London; Dr. Eggeling of the Stenographic Office, Berlin; Messrs. J. Bettos of the Prime Minister's Office, Athens; H. Creighton of the Society for Cultural Relations with U.S.S.R., London; F. Fabritius of the Stenographic Office, Finnish Parliament, Helsinki; A.

Van Gelderen, Shorthand Tutor, Amsterdam; N. Gracie, B.A., LL.B., Deputy Principal, Rapid Results College, Durban; A. Lundman of Melinska Stenografförbundet, Stockholm; H. Matzinger, Shorthand Tutor, Zurich; J. Suchanek, Secretary Czechoslovak Embassy, London; D. Dalmau, Director of Belpost-Tecnopost, Barcelona; the British Museum, Guildhall Library, Italian and Spanish Institutes, London; Hove and Wimbledon Public Libraries and all the consulates in London.

The older facts are mainly from the Shorthand histories by Melin (Swedish), Johnen (German), the Dictionary of National Biography (English) and the proceedings of the last International Shorthand Congress.

Chapter I

Development of Handwriting

Before dealing with the most important shorthand systems past and present, it is advisable to consider briefly the origin and development of handwriting.

The summary on page 9 shows approximately the development of handwriting followed by that of shorthand. Man's first attempt at writing consisted of only crude drawings of ideas. However, in the course of time these sketches became necessarily so simplified that they were meaningless to the untaught. The first picture writing was found among the Sumerians of Southern Mesopotamia and from approximately there the human race spread over the world. Therefore, at a later date picture writing (hieroglyphics) appeared also in Egypt. This was then simplified still further by the Phoenicians who reduced the many signs to 22, written from right to left. Later it was found easier to proceed from left to right, as the right hand does not cover up what it has written, nor does drawing the hand along meet with so much resistance as pushing it. Cadmus introduced these signs into Greece where they were slightly changed. The first sign, alpha, was still almost recognizable as derived from the sketch of a bull's head (Aleph) and together with the second, beta, has caused the whole series of letters to be called "the alphabet." The Latin alphabet developed from the Greek. Meanwhile those tribes who had wandered eastward under less favorable circumstances did not reduce their picture writing to an alphabet. Chinese and its offspring, Japanese, for instance, still consist of difficult word pictures.

There are over a thousand languages spoken in the world today, many of which have not been reduced to writing at all. The Bible, or at least part thereof, has been translated into about nine hundred languages.

Development of Handwriting and Shorthand

B.C.
3000   Sumerian Pictographic
             Egyptian Hieroglyphic
             Chinese Picture Writing
             Phoenician Alphabet
             Hebrew. Arabic
             Greek Alphabet
             Slavonic. Runic
             Latin Alphabet

Cursive Shorthand

103   Tiro

Geometric Shorthand

A.D.		
1600		J. Willis
1786		Taylor
1818	Gabelsberger	
1837		Pitman
1888		Gregg
1897	Stolze-Schrey	
1917		Dutton

Chapter II

Ancient Shorthand

Though some form of shorthand was known in the Orient and Xenophon used an ancient Greek system to write down Socrates' memoirs, it was in the Roman Empire that stenography first became widely employed. As at that time one usually wrote on wax tablets, the ancient shorthand systems would mostly have been lost, had not signs been written also on parchment, paper or stone. Various Roman tombstones have shorthand inscriptions.

The first important inventor of a system in Latin was Marcus Tullius Tiro (born 103 B.C. at Arpinum in Latium), Cicero's secretary. On the whole his method was a shortened longhand with the subsequent addition of diacriticals (usually dots). These are common in Oriental writing, where they often serve as a substitute for vowels; and one could include the accents and the like of European languages. Incidentally, an apostrophe has been aptly described as a "literary tombstone set up in memory of a departed letter." Tiro's shorthand, the most widely known at the time, lasted also the longest—about a thousand years, longer than any modern system so far. It lingered on until the Middle Ages and has played a part especially in perfecting the cursive systems of modern times. Tiro's method is cursive.

"Cursive," meaning literally "running," is usually the description of shorthand more or less derived from longhand as distinct from geometrical shorthand which is based on a geometrical figure such as a circle, oval, straight line or a combination of these. "Cursive" is a better term than the alternative expressions, common in English-speaking countries, "graphic" or "script," as these two words, of course, mean literally "written."

From examples of Tiro's shorthand it would appear that perhaps the best of his abbreviations from longhand is the simplified *N*. In fact, this has been retained in leading German systems today and in the present methods influenced by them in Greece (Adamopoulo), Holland (Groote) and Russia (Sokolov).

At the time of Christ, under Emperor Augustus, there was much interest in the development of shorthand. Although Tiro did not issue a shorthand textbook, he compiled a shorthand dictionary. Vipsanius (Agrippa), a Roman military leader, enlarged the system and then Filagrius issued a textbook of it with a classification into roots, prefixes and suffixes. Subsequently Aquila and Seneca made further improvements. Shorthand was used in the Roman army not merely to save time but also because it served as a secret writing unintelligible to the lower ranks and the conquered peoples. It was employed in the Senate to record speeches, and in the courts. Relays of stenographers took down the orations if they were too long. History records that when Metellus, a centurion converted to Christianity who refused to be conscripted any more, was condemned to death, a Christian shorthand writer reporting the case threw the wax tablets at the judge who then imposed the death penalty on the stenographer as well. Emperor Titus, Julius Caesar and later on many of the early bishops were accomplished shorthand writers. A stenographer received a better salary than the average teacher of those days.

Seeing that with Tiro's method it was unimportant whether the strokes were thick or thin, his system is a light-line one; that is to say, of even thickness.

Bishop Cassienus of Imola (Italy), a severe shorthand teacher, was stabbed to death by his pupils with their stylos during a persecution of Christians. He was proclaimed patron saint of shorthand writers in 1952.

Chapter III

Old British Geometrical Systems

When England had settled down to Norman rule after 1066, Thomas à Becket, who was born in the City of London and became Archbishop of Canterbury, encouraged research into Tiro's shorthand, known also as the Tironian or Seneca's Notes. It is assumed that a monk, John of Tilbury, was employed in that connection. This sufficed to stimulate the invention of British shorthand systems.

And so, slightly influenced by the Tironian Notes, Timothe Bright was one of the first to design an English system. Born in Cambridge and later a parson in Methley, he issued one in 1588 consisting of straight lines, circles and half circles. In consideration of his dedicating the system to

Queen Elizabeth I, he was granted the monopoly of publishing it for fifteen years. His intention was that it should become international in that his signs, each representing a whole word, should mean the same thing in every language just as a plus sign in arithmetic does. That is why he called his shorthand "Characterie." Though possible with a small vocabulary, it becomes unworkable with a large one. His word signs had a geometrical basis. However, most shorthand systems employ a limited number of word signs for the most frequently used words instead of writing these out in full shorthand.

The next geometrical system of note was that of John Willis, a London clergyman born about 1575, whom one could describe as the father of modern shorthand. He designed a complete shorthand alphabet, and in addition provided diacriticals as alternatives for vowels, placing the diacritical dots in their musical order on a descending scale (*i, e, a, o, u*), thus showing that in those days vowels in English were already pronounced in the Continental manner. In later life he seems to have tried to derive his shorthand alphabet from the longhand alphabet; but unfortunately his son, who had assisted him, died prematurely and Willis the elder gave up improving the system. The church of St. Mary Bothaw, where he was rector, was close to the lodging of the famous circumnavigator, Sir Francis Drake, and the Steel (Staple) Yard of the Hanseatic Traders or Easterlings after whom the word "Sterling" is named. It is a pity that the whole historic site was covered by a railway station (Cannon Street) about one hundred years ago.

A great advantage of shorthand systems with a complete alphabet is that any word may also be written literally in shorthand if necessary, and not just phonetically (as sounded) or by resorting to longhand. This ensures absolute accuracy when called for. In placing his diacritical dots in their natural, musical, instead of alphabetical order (*a, e, i, o, u*), Willis rightly used the most highly placed dot to indicate the then highest-sounding vowel (*i*) pronunced "ee." This coincides with the duration of pronunciation in that it requires more effort to pronounce a high vowel than a low one. Therefore, the former, allowing the stenographer more writing time, can be placed farthest away from the line. In many systems even today this principle has been reversed! Surely a backward step.

Just before Bright's monopoly was due to expire, Willis published anonymously, about 1600, his first book *Art of Stenography,* thus first using the word "stenography" for shorthand. His system was such an improvement on existing ones that it was adapted to at least one foreign language, Dutch.

Considerably influenced by Willis was Thomas Shelton, born 1601, who called his own system "Short Writing" and eventually with alterations "Zeiglographia." Pepys wrote his well-known diary in Shelton's shorthand, wherein, as an eyewitness, he describes the horrors of the Great Plague and the Great Fire of London. Moreover, in Pepys's notes one finds, in England, for the first time the expression "longhand" as opposed to "shorthand." Shelton devised a number of useful signs, each expressing a combination of two or more consonants that frequently occur together in English, such as *NG, SH, TH*. His method was adapted to Swedish by Johan Swan, who on returning to Sweden was knighted there as reward for his adaptation.

Charles Ramsay, a Scot, produced from existing British systems a method which he adapted to Latin. His French version, called "Tachéographie," was in turn rendered into Swedish; there was also a German adaptation. Ramsay's Latin shorthand was used by Van Swieten, physician to

Empress Maria Theresa of Austria, and as late as 1727 at Leyden University.

Meanwhile Jeremiah Rich, who fought under Cromwell in the Civil War, improved an existing method. His "Semography" was adapted to Welsh much later by Robert Everett, a clergyman who died in 1875.

The Reformation had given the greatest impetus to shorthand since Tiro's days, as the dissolution of the monasteries released specimens of Tironian Notes for wider study. Moreover, people learned shorthand so as to take down the sermons of the new preachers and copy parts of the Bible, translated from the Latin, lest some potentate appear who might wish to confiscate the translations. Thus Daniel Defoe, author of *Robinson Crusoe*, transcribed part of the Bible into shorthand. As sermons were usually slow, the cumbersome geometrical systems of the day sufficed for a while; but they required a good education in order to guess doubtful words correctly when reading shorthand.

A much easier system was that of the London doctor, John Byrom, who was born in Manchester on February 29, 1690. No funds were available to publish his textbook until after his death, and today he is more likely to be remembered as the author of the Christmas hymn, "Christians Awake, Salute the Happy Morn." John and Charles Wesley were among his pupils, and his system reached America where even Indians learned it. Moreover, he opened shorthand clubs in coffee houses of Cambridge, London and Manchester. His alphabet lacks vowels: these are indicated by diacriticals.

At about the same time as Byrom's system, appeared also that of James Weston who was buried in St. Bride's the "Journalists' Church," in the City of London.

A further system, Mason's, was altered by a schoolmaster Thomas Gurney, founder of the present firm of shorthand writers, W. B. Gurney & Sons, London. His shorthand was used by the novelist, Charles Dickens, when he was a reporter in the House of Commons. It was named "Brachygraphy."

At that time even a small shorthand textbook, without any oral tuition, was very expensive, Gurney charging a guinea for quite a small book in 1750 (about five pounds at today's values).

Whereas British systems so far were very short-lived in comparison with the one thousand years' use of Tiro's shorthand, we now come to one that lasted in Britain for about a century and forms the backbone of many present methods, especially in Belgium, France, Spain, Portugal, South America and the Orient. This was the system of Samuel Taylor, who was born near the Welsh border about 1748. Very little indeed is known of Taylor's private life, great man though he was. He traveled about teaching shorthand in order to support his two children and died in 1811 in the Pimlico quarter of London. His system, which he called the "Universal System of Stenography or Short Hand Writing," was largely based on Byrom's. It had no vowels except the diacritical dots, was fairly easy to learn and write, but difficult to read back.

Chapter IV

British Influence Abroad

Since Taylor's system was a great improvement on existing ones, it was adapted to French in 1792 by Théodore Bertin, a book dealer in Paris. Josef Danzer, an Austrian major taken prisoner during the Napoleonic Wars, learned the Taylor-Bertin system in Paris with a view to making it an international one. However, after he had adapted it to German and Latin, he fell at the Battle of Aspern. Stenographic entries in Beethoven's notebooks, which the composer used when he lost his hearing, are written in Danzer's adaptation of Taylor's system. Marti, inventor of the fountain pen, rendered the method into Spanish; his son, into Portuguese. Amanti adapted it to Italian, and Silverstople to Swedish. France had, incidentally, a few systems already, such as the geometrical method of Jacques Cossard, a priest.

The idea of a shorthand system adaptable to all languages is practicable despite the view sometimes held that stenographic methods are best for that language in which they were invented. After all, Latin longhand is gradually being adopted by most countries, and the old notation in music is used successfully all over the world along with Arabic and Roman numerals, to mention only a few international methods of thought expression.

Karl Mosengeil, a German theologian, published a geometrical system based to a large extent on Taylor's and seems to have been among the first since Tiro to pay more attention to the design of special signs for prefixes and suffixes.

A year later Karl Horstig, likewise a German clergyman, modified Mosengeil's system. The latter considered Horstig's alterations an improvement and adopted them himself. It is related that one Karl Winter when only sixteen wrote Horstig's system holding in his right hand about a dozen goose quills.

Meanwhile in France Conen de Prépéan developed a method influenced by Taylor's which in turn had some effect on that of Aimé Paris, a lawyer, born at Quimper in 1798. Paris' system, which was more original, found its way also to Belgium, Holland and the French-speaking part of Switzerland. It induced two priests, E. and A. Delaunay, to make improvements which in turn influenced Emile Duployé, born at Liesse in 1833. Duployé, who gave up practicing as a priest in order to devote himself to shorthand, died in 1912. He had been assisted in his work by his brothers Aldoric, Gustave and Jules, and his system spread to other French-speaking countries, including Canada, where Pater-Le-Jeune, a missionary, taught it to Indians as their first and for a while only method of writing. The system was adapted to Armenian, Chinese, Hebrew, Japanese, Persian, Russian, Arabic (Syrian), etc.

Lars Hierta, founder of the newspaper *Aftonbladet*, introduced a system in Sweden based on those of De Prépéan and Paris. Such was and is the far-reaching influence of Taylor outside Britain.

A system that commanded some attention in England soon after Taylor's was that of James Lewis, who was born in Gloucestershire in 1786. He was a friend of Sir Walter Scott, the novelist, and founded a Society of Reporters.

Although British influence on shorthand abroad was predominantly geometrical, some of the British cursive systems no doubt had their effect also. Rather interesting too is the method of Kristian Grabergh of Stockholm issued in 1731 (Tachygraphia). There one finds traces of a good beginning to a cursive system which attempts the placing of consonants above or below the line in substitution of high- or low-sounding vowels respectively.

Such raising, lowering or distancing farther to the right of consonants is known as positioning. This had already been slightly attempted in England by a postmaster Folkingham (born 1575 at Helpringham), a schoolmaster Coles (born 1640 at Northampton) and Nicolas in his "Thoographia" published in 1692. It rightly attempts to view the recording of speech from a musical angle; and this was perfected later in Germany especially by Schrey.

Incidentally, Duployé quite rightly was a staunch supporter of the free choice of systems, convinced that only by competition between systems could an ideal one evolve. In this he was supported by the journalist and gifted shorthand historian Albert Navarre.

Chapter V.

Growth of the Cursive Systems

As Europe became industrialized, the demand for stenographers in business houses and thus for easier shorthand systems arose. England on her island had remained comparatively untouched by the great Continental political and religious upheavals and had been able to produce many shorthand systems, mostly geometrical. However, they all presupposed a high standard of education and a very long training in the system.

And so Franz Gabelsberger, born in Munich in 1789, turning away from geometrical methods set about developing a simple cursive system. Gabelsberger, whom one might describe as the greatest inventor of a shorthand system, was the son of a musical instrument maker. On the early death of his father, Franz became a chorister, being brought up by a monastery where he learned Latin. This became most useful to him in his later fruitful study of the Tironian Notes, a study which he encouraged in others and himself pursued until his death. However, Tiro's shorthand was scarcely known to Gabelsberger when he laid the foundation of his system. He made a living as correspondent for various authorities and gradually evolved from longhand a shorthand system of his own. He thus took up the inheritance of centuries of Latin longhand characters which had already proved their superiority over Oriental writing. He called his system "Speech-sign art."

Already in England, for instance, a priest Simon Bordley, having learned Mason's geometrical system, had published a cursive one in 1787. This could be written either upright or slanting to the right and consisted in part of only the backbone or downstroke of longhand letters, which could be written either disconnected (like Greek characters) or linked together by a hairstroke (like Latin longhand characters). The system was light-line. Bordley, by the way, was one of those who designed a shorthand system for music.

Then Roe, Adams and Oxley, likewise in England, published some little-known cursive systems. However, none of the methods in existence could in any way approach the great advance made by Gabelsberger.

It had become apparent to him that some of the vowels and diphthongs could be omitted and yet be expressed not only by positioning the consonant up or down or to the right, but also by sometimes thickening its downstroke. Positioning and thickening dispense with hooks, loops, circles and diacriticals and, in the case of diacriticals, avoid lifting the hand away from the paper and bringing it down again.

Influenced perhaps by Tiro, Gabelsberger sometimes intersected shorthand characters. This means that one sign crosses another, thus producing a third.

Gabelsberger's system shows a neatness and beauty of outline which is unsurpassed. He himself wrote neatly and quickly, though handicapped by the disadvantages of the writing materials of those days. Not until later did the pliable and finer steel nib and good pencils become available.

Incidentally, although fountain pens with fine, pure gold nibs are very suitable for shorthand, those with hard, gold-saving iridium tips are not, neither are ball-point pens. Of pencils, the writer has found a hexagonal, soft finely pointed at both ends, best; and of shorthand notebooks those which open out perfectly flat. When writing, it is better to hold the pencil almost at right angles to the paper.

Thanks to improved writing materials, which are taken for granted nowadays, later systems could make better use of downstroke thickening, where desirable, than Gabelsberger did. However, his system enjoyed a spontaneous, unequaled success even before he died aged 59 in Munich in 1849. Physically weak, he had not been conscripted by Napoleon for the disastrous Russian campaign in which his brother had perished. In 1943 an air raid destroyed the Gabelsberger Museum in Munich, and little was saved. Among many souvenirs, it had contained the cardboard cover from which horizontal strips had been cut so that Gabelsberger could take down dictation in an unlit coach at night from Prince Oettingen-Wallerstein on the twenty-mile journeys over rough roads to the prince's residence. Another memento was a bronze plate inscribed "Gabelsberger" from a railway engine named after him. Such was the popularity of his system. It spread to the German-speaking part of Switzerland and to Austria. As its success became known, delegates arrived from the governments in Scandinavia, Finland and Russia to learn the system and adapt it to their own languages.

Denmark had sent a representative also to France with a view to importing a French system inspired by Taylor. However, Gabelsberger's proved more suitable so that it was adapted to Danish by David Dessau, who was on the staff of the *Berlingske Tidende* and died in 1893. Kurik rendered it into Esthonian; Polinski adapted it to Polish; Professor Heger to Czech and the main Slav languages.

In 1922, however, as a result of the First Congress of Slav Stenographers, held in Prague in 1891, Czechoslovakia adopted a cursive system created by Dr. Alois Herout and Ing. Svojmir Mikulik which has been adapted to Bulgarian, English, French, German, Hungarian, Italian, Russian, Serbian, Spanish and Esperanto.

Meanwhile Josef Mindler introduced Gabelsberger's shorthand into Greece; and Heinrich Noe brought it to Italy, where in 1928 Mussolini made it the Italian national system. Dr. Lars Nervius' (Nevanlinna) revised Finnish version of Gabelsberger's system is the one most used in

Finland today. There were adaptations also to Dutch, Hungarian, Norwegian, Rumanian, Turkish, Chinese and other languages. Dostoievsky dictated his novels to a lady secretary who wrote Gabelsberger's shorthand adapted to Russian.

The superiority of Gabelsberger's system caused most of the Continent north, east and south of the Rhine to give up geometrical systems and paved the way for other cursive methods. Before considering these, let us see what progress the geometrical systems west of the Rhine were making.

BYROM Shorthand

Alphabet
(Consonants only)

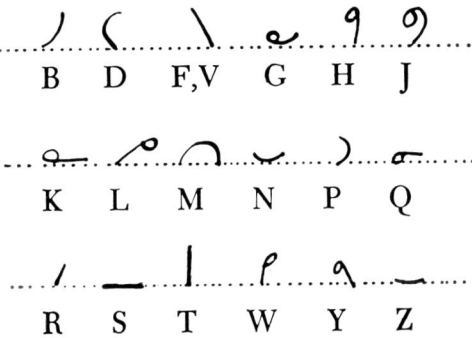

Vowel indication
(diacriticals)

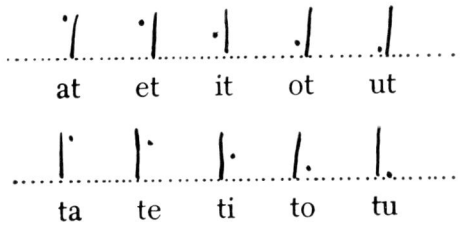

GABELSBERGER Shorthand

Alphabet
(1834)

a b c d e f g h

i j k l m n o p

qu r s t u v w x z

GREGG Shorthand

Derived from oval—
has no complete alphabet.

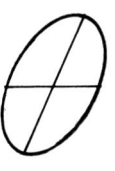

Alphabet
(Consonants only)

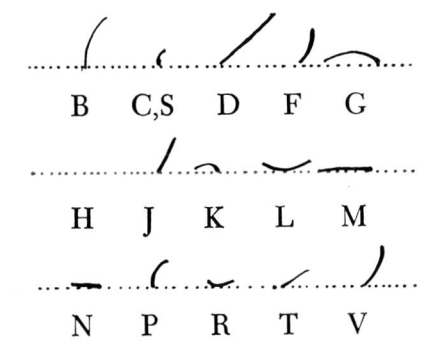

B   C,S   D   F   G

H   J   K   L   M

N   P   R   T   V

Vowel indication
(Ovals, hooks, diacriticals)

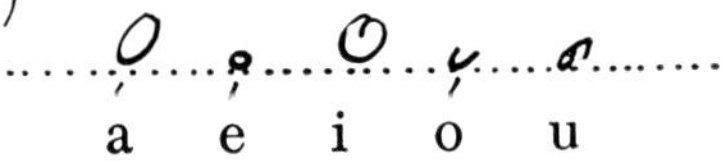

a   e   i   o   u

etc.

GROOTE Shorthand

Alphabet

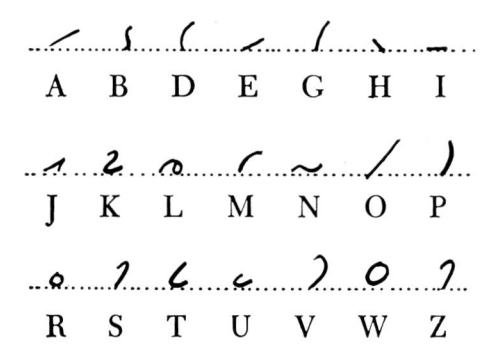

A	B	D	E	G	H	I

J	K	L	M	N	O	P

R	S	T	U	V	W	Z

PARIS Shorthand

Alphabet

A	B	C	D	E	F	G
I	J	L	M	N	O	P
R	S	T	U	V	Z	

Examples

l'avantage

l'univers

PITMAN Shorthand

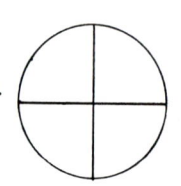

Alphabet
(Consonants only)

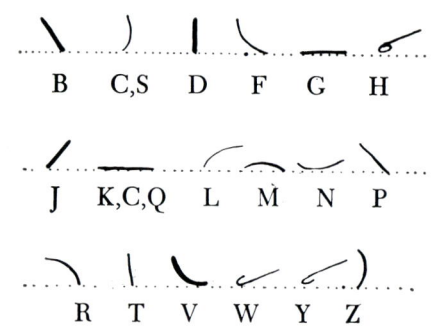

Derived from circle—
has no complete alphabet.

| B | C,S | D | F | G | H |

| J | K,C,Q | L | M | N | P |

| R | T | V | W | Y | Z |

Vowel indication
(diacriticals)

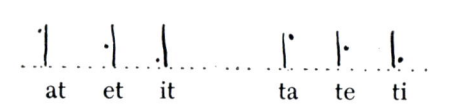

at   et   it   ta   te   ti

etc.

STOLZE-SCHREY Shorthand

Derived from longhand, has complete alphabet.

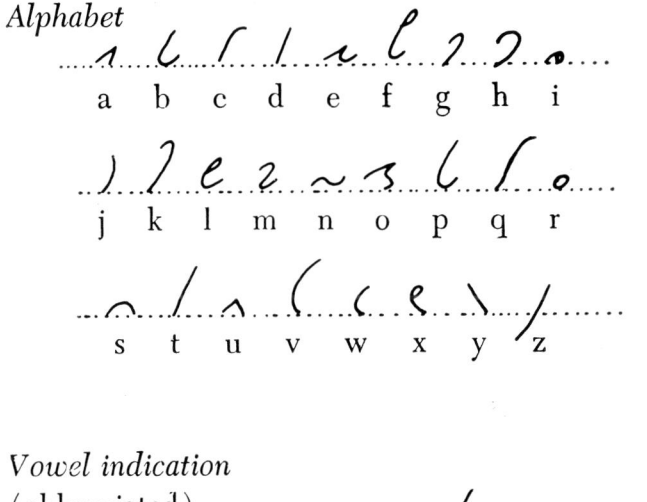

Alphabet

a b c d e f g h i

j k l m n o p q r

s t u v w x y z

Vowel indication
(abbreviated)

bat bet bit lot loot

etc.

above line in
reporting style
(further
abbreviation)

TIRO Shorthand

Alphabet

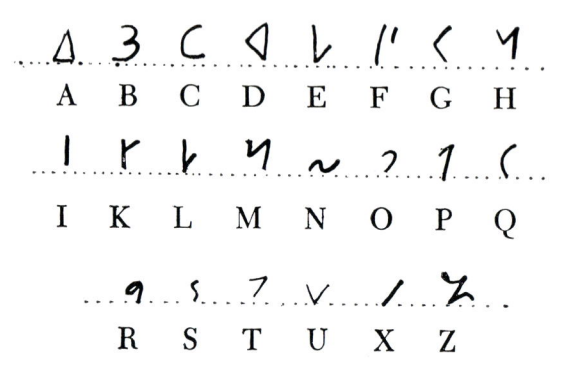

Δ	3	C	◁	レ	/'	﹤	Ч
A	B	C	D	E	F	G	H

l	ʳ	ⱱ	Ч	∼	?	7	(
I	K	L	M	N	O	P	Q

۹	ς	7	∨	╱	ⱬ
R	S	T	U	X	Z

Signs for
Combined consonants   ✕   ⼃

                 CH   PH   etc.

Word-signs

7   Λ   3⁻   ʃ   7   ∼

INDEX ALIUS BREVIS SE TE NON

                                          etc

Chapter VI

Modern British Geometrical Methods

In 1813 Isaac Pitman was born at Trowbridge in England. He became a teacher in one of the Church schools before most of them were nationalized. Unlike Gabelsberger, his main interest was not shorthand but spelling reform, a subject to which he was devoted until his death in 1897, about three years after being knighted by Queen Victoria for his contribution to shorthand. Pitman had learned Taylor's system, and this slightly influenced his own which he called "Stenographic Sound-Hand."

As a teacher of elementary school children, who lack that classical education which facilitates correct spelling, he wished to abolish existing English orthography and, instead, spell phonetically. A vegetarian and total abstainer, he changed his religious views also and became a Swedenborgian. Having to resign from teaching in Church schools, he opened a private school, but gave this up in order to publish *Spelling Reform*, which ran him into debt.

Though phonetic spelling in shorthand was not unknown, his spelling reform publicity drew attention to his shorthand, in which he was assisted by his brothers, one of whom spread the system from London, another in Australia, and a third in North America.

Pitman's method is based on the circle, the individual signs being parts thereof (radius, etc.), so that unlike ordinary handwriting, which slopes to the right, it has to be written upright. Whereas geometrical systems so far had been light-line, Pitman thickened certain strokes to distinguish heavy-sounding consonants from their lighter-sounding counterparts. For instance, his *B* is like his *P* but thickened. Actually, it needs more effort to pronounce *P* than *B*. Consequently, as *P's* duration of pronunciation is longer, the stenographer can take more time in writing it and, therefore, *P* should have been thickened. In order to express vowels and diphthongs Pitman had to resort to employing diacriticals in sixteen variations.

His method, like Gabelsberger's, has been in use for over a century and has been adapted to Afrikaans, Arabic, Armenian, Dutch, French, Gaelic (Irish), German, Hebrew, Hindi, Italian, Japanese, Persian, Spanish, etc. Yet Pitman never achieved, any more than Gabelsberger did, that almost complete monopoly which for about a hundred years was exercised by the mysterious Taylor. Strange to say, during Pitman's lifetime an echo of Taylor's influence came back to England from abroad as follows.

In France, a friend of Duployé's (whose system had been considerably influenced by Taylor) was a Scot, John Sloan; and Sloan adapted Duployé's method to English under the name of Sloan-Duployan, thus reviving Taylor's influence in Britain.

In this Sloan was assisted by Thomas Malone (born in Dublin, 1847) who, however, was not satisfied with the system and evolved from it a "script" method of his own; an improvement, but really still geometrical being based on an oval. The system, sloping like ordinary handwriting to the right, was once again light-line and for vowels and diphthongs used large and small ovals, hooks and diacriticals. It is known as "Script Shorthand" or "Clark's Shorthand," as still taught in Clark's Commercial Colleges. Malone, who was undoubtedly a shorthand genius, died in London in 1925, where he was laid to rest in Highgate cemetery not far from the grave of Karl Marx.

One of Malone's helpers was John Gregg, likewise born in Ireland, at Rockcorry in 1867. Gregg started as a writer in a lawyer's office in Glasgow and with the aid of his brother published a textbook in 1888 of "Light-line Phonography," which is similar to Malone's system. As, however, the methods of Pitman, Sloan-Duployan and Malone were popular in England then, Gregg found more pupils in America, where his system predominates. Later it achieved much success in England too. Gregg was aided by his wife, a former Pitman teacher. However, like Pitman and many others, Malone and Gregg lost sight of the importance of the duration of pronunciation in designing their signs.

Dr. Gregg, having received an honorary degree for his valuable contribution to shorthand, died in America in 1948. His system has been adapted to several languages, including Hebrew (about 1955) by Bar-Kama (Kempinski). The shorthand writer of the late President Roosevelt of the Second World War was a Gregg writer as are several leading speedwriters in the U.S.A., where so much importance is attached to speed records as a means of advertising typewriters or shorthand systems.

The latest well-known geometrical method in English-speaking countries is that of Reginald Dutton, born in Nottingham in 1886, who was a journalist and reporter for the *Daily Telegraph*, and published his system about 1917. Following the principle of the typewriter keyboard, where letters are arranged according to their frequency of use (the most-used being in the middle), he gave the most often employed letters—at least in English—the most easily written signs, while using hooks for vowels and thickening some of the signs.

Incidentally, though one grows accustomed to the present arrangement of the typewriter keyboard, expert typists often doubt whether it is the ideal one. Personally, as a touch typist (and pianist and violinist) I feel that typewriter manufacturers could make better machines if they were to invite suggestions from typists. Many an employer, who has not even learned touch typing, expects first-class work from a typist with a poor machine. Under such circumstances no concert pianist, for instance, would condescend to play a single note.

However, it requires research into the letter frequencies of every language before a shorthand "keyboard" individual for each language, let alone one common for all, is evolved. Therefore, it is much more natural and simpler to view the recording of speech from a musical angle, allowing for duration of pronunciation and being aided by inherited tendencies.

In 1949 Percy Harwood published *English Shorthand* at Brighton, a combination of the systems of Malone and Gregg. Of special interest, however, are the attempts in English-speaking countries to design cursive systems in more recent times. We shall refer to these later.

Chapter VII

Perfecting the Cursive Methods

At about the same time as Gabelsberger was designing his system, Heinrich Stolze (born in Berlin, 1798) planned one on similar lines. When Stolze was still studying theology his father died. He gave up his studies and in order to support his mother entered a fire insurance office. In order to cope with the large amount of writing, he set about condensing longhand, eventually becoming a shorthand teacher and president of the Stenographic Bureau of the Prussian Chamber of Deputies. Like Gabelsberger, Stolze had benefited by a classical education, but aimed at a better association of ideas than the former in designing the shorthand alphabet. By "association of ideas" I mean as regards shorthand that each letter of the shorthand alphabet should as far as possible be derived from the corresponding letter, capital or small, of the longhand alphabet, which, as we have seen, has come down to us from word pictures. Thus Stolze takes, for instance, (as did Gabelsberger) the last loop of the small longhand *M* as his shorthand *M*, uses a simplified *N* (like our illustration of Tiro's) for the shorthand *N*, the stem of the straight, German (Gothic) longhand *T* for a shorthand *T*, and expresses *D*, related in sound to *T*, by a downstroke half the size of that for *T*. And so at the same time the length of the shorthand sign corresponds generally to the duration of pronunciation. By contrast, Gabelsberger's *D*, for example, unfortunately resembles a small longhand *E* or *L*. This is because he deliberately avoided giving related sounds such as *D* and *T* similar signs, fearing they might be confused. In this he was overanxious and handicapped his system, especially as some of the German dialects (e. g., Saxon) reverse the pronunciation of, for example, *D* and *T* in any case. The advantage of association of ideas, particularly in the case of related sounds, is too great to be purposely suppressed. Association of ideas includes the musical positioning of shorthand consonants so that by placing them high or low they not only fulfill their function as consonants but at the same time serve as vowels or diphthongs. By thickening the consonant's downstroke for the longer sounds generally, the remaining vowels or diphthongs (with or without positioning) are obtained. There is little doubt, therefore, that the most natural and logical method of recording speech by shorthand is, supported by inherited tendencies and association of ideas, to consider sounds from the musical aspect and their duration of pronunciation.

Stolze aimed at this in his system, but it was not until the later similar one of Schrey was linked to it, producing the Stolze-Schrey method, that a system resulted which many authorities (and I) consider most closely approaches the ideal.

I remember when my mother was mistress of the old Infants School of St. Dunstan's, Fleet Street, in the City of London, she had a boy who had been rejected as ineducable by three state schools. He could not learn to read. Recollecting my own childhood, I knew that the pictures illustrating the alphabet would probably go against the sense of association of ideas. Therefore, I drew the boy a chart on which the small "*a*" formed part of the picture of an apple; "*t*" was a tree with two branches; "*v*" formed the open neck of a vest, and so on. This was a better association of ideas than with the common illustrations of, say, Alfred for "*a*", Tommy for "*t*", and Vera for "*v*", even if those persons were depicted in an attitude resembling the shape of the desired letter. Where there is no reasonable association of ideas children have to resort to the more difficult "look-and-say" method of reading. At any rate, the ineducable one suddenly learned to read through my unilateral "correspondence course."

Stolze's system became the leading one in the Reichstag and Northern Germany. It was adapted to other languages, particularly Dutch, and introduced into the Dutch colonies, South Africa, and elsewhere. Count Tolstoy dictated his works to a lady secretary who wrote a Russian adaptation of Stolze's system. There was also a little-known adaptation to English by John Thompson in 1863, entitled "Shorthand swift as Speech." In 1888 Heinrich Richter, a member of the Shorthand Society in London, adapted Gabelsberger's method to English. However, as Britain was more interested in the lively competition between British geometrical systems, the then two leading Continental cursive systems (Gabelsberger's and Stolze's) never secured a fair trial in England. In 1867 Stolze passed away and was interred in a

Berlin cemetery, where his epitaph reads: "Your best monument is your work."

As his system and Gabelsberger's had much in common, attempts were made by, for instance, Heinrich Stephan, later postmaster general in Germany, to merge the two.

Leopold Arends, born of German parents near Vilna, developed a method based on Stolze's by converting it into a light-line one. Extra flourishes had to be introduced to make up for positioning and thickening. The result was not very good, but his system in adaptation was popular for a time in Scandinavia and other Baltic states. Arends' main service to shorthand was that he stressed the importance of the knowledge of that art to anyone who has much writing to do and, by remaining loyal to the cursive systems, erred on the right side. Moreover, he helped to pave the way for the adaptation of later cursive systems to East and North European languages so that the leading system in, for instance, Russia today (Sokolov's) is likewise cursive and widely used.

Meanwhile in 1831 someone known as "Lady Sophy Scott" (there is some doubt as to who the "lady" was) published a most peculiar geometrical method in Vienna, with diacriticals for vowels.

It was too difficult; but for the first time, at least in more modern times, "Lady Scott" emphasized the advantage of placing diacritical dots not in alphabetical but but in musical or natural order on a descending scale. It is now so obvious to anyone with musical feeling that one wonders why no one, apart from John Willis, seems to have considered it important. When in 1837, six years after "Lady Scott's" publication, Pitman issued his, the original vowel scale of his diacriticals (though not so logical musically as hers) was more in accordance with the musical or natural order than it is today. He changed his vowel scale in 1857 to its present form in spite of strong objection from his brother Benn in America and from Thomas Reed, a Pitman stenographer and founder of the present firm T. A. Reed & Co., shorthand writers, London. The change was a step backward.

As regards herself "Lady Scott" wrote: "The world will probably never know my real name; but the name 'Sophy Scott' shall still for many years to come pass unforgotten from mouth to mouth." Rather prophetic. Here again, therefore, we have a personality of genius whose private life, like Taylor's, still remains wrapped in mystery. In 1929 an Austrian shorthand-research worker,

Dr. Ernst Weizmann, held that "Sophy Scott" was a man with a sense of humor named Adam Würth.

We now come to one of the greatest men in the history of shorthand, Ferdinand Schrey. Born 1850 at Wuppertal-Elberfeld and son of a businessman, he became one too, owning a small factory, and was one of the first to introduce and sell the typewriter, which had then just arrived from America. From 1885 onward he devoted himself to shorthand and his typewriter business in Berlin. Like Pitman, he was a vegetarian and total abtstainer. The widowed Empress of Germany (born in England), rather unwisely from a social point of view and despite opposition from conservatives, who believed that woman's place is in the home, encouraged the entry of young women into offices as shorthand-typists, a secretarial vocation which until then had been very efficiently exercised only by educated men. As the young women generally had less education than the men and had no desire to study a difficult shorthand system, which they would normally not use once they married, Schrey, noticing their difficulty in learning such comparatively simple systems as Gabelsberger's and Stolze's, improved Gabelsberger's by means of Stolze's.

He was influenced partly by Faulmann, born

in 1875 in the old university town of Halle on the Saale (widely known as the birthplace of the composer Handel). Faulmann, a typesetter, had himself designed an excellent cursive system in the hope that it would do away with longhand altogether.

Schrey positioned his consonants more according to musical feeling as already expressed by the old notation of music. Any musician will confirm that Curwen's Tonic Sol-Fa method of writing music without raising or lowering (known especially in English-speaking countries) does not readily influence eye and ear and that the usual and more natural, old notation is superior. It must be admitted, of course, that even in shorthand it is possible to learn almost any system and with practice achieve a record; for there were well-known speedwriters even of Tiro's shorthand.

Based on Dr. Mantzel's draft, the systems of Stolze and Schrey were merged and submitted for approval to Oskar Henke, headmaster of a secondary school; Professor Adolf Socin, head of the Gabelsberger Society in Switzerland; and Christian Johnen (born 1862), a barrister and the world's greatest shorthand historian. All these Gabelsberger students agreed that the Stolze-Schrey system was a great improvement.

Johnen and Schrey died in 1938 after the Stolze-Schrey system had become the leading one in Germany, was introduced into Switzerland (where it occupies a prominent position today) and other German-speaking districts, and was adapted to Danish, Dutch, English, Esthonian, French, Ancient Greek, Italian, Latin, Latvian, Lithuanian, Norwegian, Polish, Russian, Spanish and Esperanto. In some cases there are, of course, more than one adaptation to the same language.

Incidentally, Waern of Sweden, who died in 1931, made a very good adaptation of Schrey's own system to Swedish. Had he been able to afford greater publicity, the adaptation would probably have become Sweden's national system. However, the light-line cursive method of the famous Swedish historian of shorthand, Olaf Melin, influenced by German cursive systems predominates there. Melin (1861-1940), a professional soldier, concentrated on shorthand and shorthand history when he retired as colonel.

It is noteworthy that in Eastern Europe—where shorthand is further encouraged today over the wireless—women have been prominent adapters, especially of the Stolze-Schrey system, to the languages there. Mrs. Balczynska adapted it to Polish in 1919, while Wanda Schröder issued an Esthonian version in 1918, and Emma Gaber adapted it to Latvian in 1922. Other adapters were Margareta Kilz (1923) and Lilly Puren (1927).

By contrast, west of the Rhine and especially in America and England, where aided by the influence of suffragettes they became shorthand-typists in larger numbers, women have not distinguished themselves as adapters to foreign languages. No doubt they have enough to do in mastering the more difficult geometrical systems, and Schrey had foreseen this.

Of the adaptations of the Stolze-Schrey system to foreign languages those of Heinrich Matzinger, Zürich, should be mentioned. His adaptations show a great similarity to the German original.

Born in London in 1904 and being bilingual, I had no difficulty in adapting the Stolze-Schrey method from my father's language, German, into my mother tongue, English, when I appreciated that system's advantages over the predominant methods in England. I had learned the system voluntarily at the high school in Tangermünde on the Elbe, a former imperial capital of Germany and the Holy Roman Empire (before the Hohenzollerns removed to what is now Berlin) on the eastern frontier, when Germany extended, as the poet Walter von der Vogelweide described it, only "from the Rhine to the Elbe." I adapted the Stolze-Schrey method to English in 1930 on the advice of the late Mr. Pfaendler, manager of the employment department of the Swiss Mercantile Society, London, whose speed test I successfully passed in German and in my English adaptation. As the latter contains much of the system's advanced or reporting style, it is very time-saving. It is better to know the reporting style of a system and incorporate that in the foreign adaptation. The textbook of my adaptation is in the form of a self-tutor with hints for shorthand-typists.

In 1925 the leading German systems were merged into the Unified German Shorthand. It is the considered opinion of many authorities, including my own, that the merger was a backward step, at least for the Stolze-Schrey system, the supporters of which offered more opposition than did the Gabelsberger supporters; since the Unified Shorthand consists mainly of Gabelsberger's signs with their disadvantages. The underlying reason for unification may well have been the political influence of the German authorities. Since the German army encouraged its officers to learn shorthand not only for the quicker recording of messages but also for use after return to civilian life, it was desirable that only one system should be used, at least in the armed forces. When Prussia was still predominant in Germany, the Stolze-Schrey system prevailed—already on account of its merits—in the Reichstag, the Post Office, the State Railway and the fighting services. However, when Germany became a republic, the government favored a merger of systems, which was furthered also by the later governments.

As, however, the Stolze-Schrey system is widely taught in Switzerland and continues to live also in its foreign adaptations, it is now reviving in Germany and other parts of Europe.

The Unified Shorthand was introduced into Austria and the then Free State of Danzig (1926), but the Second World War handicapped its adaptation to foreign languages. However it has influenced the recent Greek method of Adomopoulo.

About 1926 a unification of German-inspired systems took place also in Hungary; and Dr. Ernst Träger, the Hungarian Government's representative, fittingly remarked at the Fifteenth International Shorthand Congress at Budapest in 1929: "Although we have introduced the (Hungarian) unified shorthand we have no intention of displacing the other shorthand systems. In our opinion such a sweeping regulation as the introduction of unified shorthand cannot be enforced. A Government decree is in vain unless the unified shorthand takes root in most of our people through its merits and by proving its efficiency." It would indeed be a step backward if a government were inexpertly to displace an easy system by a difficult one.

Russia too set about unifying her systems at this time. A conference took place in 1925 and the Government favored Sokolov's light-line cursive system which shows German influence and has been adapted to other languages of the U.S.S.R., such as Georgian (by Leonidze), Uzbek (by Muradov), Ukrainian, etc. Prior to that, for instance at the Communist World Congress of 1922 in Moscow, adaptations of older German systems were still in use. On that occasion twelve stenographers were employed (eleven women, one man) of whom seven used Stolze's and four Gabelsberger's system adapted to Russian.

While the Stolze-Schrey system was spreading in Germany, there appeared in 1899 at Amersfoort in Holland a light-line cursive system by A. Groote (born 1859), who devoted himself to shorthand on retiring as colonel from a military career. The system, slightly influenced by the German cursive system of Scheithauer, is known also as Dutch Alphabetical Shorthand, has been adapted to a few other languages, and is one of the systems used in South Africa, where in 1950 an English cursive system appeared, designed by Judge H. Fagan of Cape Town.

Belgium, on the other hand, uses mainly French geometrical methods whereby Meysmanns adapted Aimé Paris' system to Flemish.

It is significant to note that America and England have in the last few decades continued to evolve some cursive systems, thus confirming that the geometrical methods leave much to be desired. For instance, Rundell, a London civil servant, published *Shorthand for Schools* in 1883. His cursive system was a combination of some of Pitman's and Stolze's ideas. In 1913 Oliver of Nottingham published in London, New York and Berlin his *Cursive Phonography*, a mixture of German systems. In America, Professor Dewey after designing a geometrical system swung over to the cursive methods. He traveled to Berlin, consulted Schrey and returning to America constructed "General Shorthand." Dewey issued a book of the 100,000 most frequently used words in the English language and is thus among those who have contributed to the subject of word frequency and simplified English for foreigners (Basic English). In more recent times Cima issued a cursive system in Italy. Spain and South America tend to introduce cursive systems. Prominent are those of the eminent Boada (born at St. Feliu de Guizols, 1873, died in Barcelona, 1947) and of Mr. D. Dalmau who is active in Barcelona. The considerable interest shown especially by South America in the future of shorthand is seen already from the periodical, *Boletin de Estenografia demotica,* published in Montevideo.

* * *

Reviewing the world's shorthand systems as a whole, it can be said that apart from a few curiosities such as Bayliss' perpendicular, geometrical stenography (London, 1911), written in Chinese fashion down the page instead of across it, and a few semi-shorthand methods (consisting of moderately abbreviated longhand), systems can be classified under the two main headings, cursive and geometrical, of which the former is the older. Both can be divided into light-line systems and those which allow thickening of certain strokes. Further, one distinguishes methods where consonant positioning acts as a substitute for vowels, from those expressing vowels only by means of diacriticals and/or hooks, circles, loops and ovals. Finally, there are systems with a complete alphabet and those in which, having an incomplete alphabet, one must resort to longhand where necessary. Sometimes geometrical systems are mistakenly called cursive (graphic or script), but unlike a purely cursive system they are not in any way derived from longhand. Geometrical systems have largely disappeared from countries where they used to predominate.

In view of the "shorthand" and dictating machines it is sometimes asked whether shorthand will be required in future. A few words about these machines, which no doubt have their advantages, should lead to the conviction that the educated shorthand writer will certainly always be required.

Chapter VIII

"Shorthand" Machines and Dictating Machines

As in consequence of the Second World War a scarcity of shorthand-typists arose, it happened that, say, a department head secured a shorthand-typist so that no other executive should take her first, but kept her unoccupied while he thought out his dictation. This unbusinesslike procedure could have been reduced if he had learned shorthand himself and could without delay read out his shorthand notes, which would also be useful to fall back on. As it is, one often makes use also of "shorthand" and dictating machines. However, in the case of newspaper reporters, the police and in the courts, where a machine cannot indicate who is speaking or is otherwise unsuitable, one has to employ stenographers.

The so-called "shorthand" machines are small, portable typewriters which can be rested on one's lap and type usually only capitals. Words are abbreviated in accordance with a scheme recommended by the makers of the machines, and the result is known as machine "shorthand." Recommended abbreviations have been suggested already for the ordinary typewriter. Italy, perhaps more than other countries, is responsible for developing this stenotyping machine. A continuous supply of paper is fed into it from a roll, saving the frequent insertion and withdrawal of single sheets. However, the abbreviations must afterward be decoded on an ordinary typewriter and, consequently, no time is saved.

Although one or two machines have been invented to type actual shorthand outlines, they have not been a success yet. Naturally, the touch typist would have to know the machine's particular shorthand system and this would no doubt have to be modified for the shorthand characters to be typed. Interesting possibilities exist.

A dictating machine records speech on the gramophone principle; but while a gramophone allows a slower, deeper-sounding reproduction, dictating machines usually reproduce only at the dictated speed so that a too fast dictation is unintelligible. As in any case the typist, by switching the dictating machine on and off, listens to only so much as can be conveniently typed, the person dictating cannot readily act as a pace maker and speed up the typing as he can speed up dictation with a shorthand writer. Therefore, with dictating machines too it is doubtful whether in the long run time and money are saved. Again, executives tend to secure a machine and then leave it unused while thinking of something to say, instead of dictating from shorthand notes of their own. With doubtful dictation it happens that a typist first takes down the recording in shorthand before eventually typing. In any case she should be acquainted with the subject matter and the dictating habits of the speaker, as questions cannot be addressed to and answered by a machine. A shorthand writer can, of course, during dictation remind his employer of this and that. A typist wearing earphones has to neglect important telephone and other calls.

Shorthand notebooks if dated and retained for a time, as they should be, are an orderly source of information in concise form; but paper strips from a "shorthand" machine must be taken out, folded, cut, identified, sorted and filed. This applies also to the dictation cylinders, discs, belts or wire of dictating machines. Very often these records (like the wax tablets and slates of old) are smoothed out and used again, unfortunately destroying the original record. Thus machines cause a certain amount of tedious extra work. They need maintenance and repair and are not so easily obtainable, cheap and portable as notebook and pencil. If unduly dependent on machines, one should have at least two in case one fails. As, moreover, confidential matter cannot be whispered to a machine, a special dictation room, entailing extra expense, is advisable.

Thus, although the machines mentioned have for a century not been unknown, shorthand will always be needed in the world. He who knows shorthand saves others and himself time, effort and money.

Conclusion

And now I must close this brief historical and technical review of the most important shorthand systems of the world. Shorthand is an art dating back about two thousand years; allusions to it exist in the Bible. Men and women, young and old, have furthered the art, and some have been highly honored for their services. There have been and are, of course, many more systems; but I have indicated the most important principles in the typical examples chosen. Speed is measured in words or syllables. Of the international Shorthand Congresses, the first in 1887 and the last in 1937 were both held in London; the latter in a shorthand jubilee year: It was the 50th world congress, 150 years had passed since Taylor's system appeared, 100 in the case of Pitman, and 50 with Gregg. Already, for that reason, one tended to review the past rather than consider the future. The Pitman publishers, especially, supported the congress at which representatives of many lands and several systems were present. Particular mention should be made of the Rev. A. Sims of England, Dr. and Mrs. Gregg of America, Colonel Melin of Sweden, Dr. Träger (a supporter of the free choice of systems in Hungary) and Miss Groote of Holland who represented her father Colonel Groote. Lectures were held and also an exhibition of old and new shorthand works. Finally, it was resolved to hold the next congress at Nuremberg in 1941, but unfortunately the Second World War intervened. Perhaps most interesting was the lecture of General von Glock (Hungary) on his problems in adapting Gabelsberger's system to Chinese. Morard (France) described a method in Arabic. A Bulgarian outlined three methods of electrically measuring the duration of writing shorthand signs. Lecturers from Russia and Austria described teaching methods in their countries, and so on. The Rev. Sims, a supporter of the Sloan-Duployan system (widely used in Ireland) rightly said in his speech: "In modern universities we have faculties of arts, medicine, law . . . and even divinity, but no faculty of shorthand. By 'faculty' I mean a university or its equivalent possessing the power of bestowing an academic distinction on those who have by intellectual achievement contributed to the domain of learning. How strange that the great art of shorthand with its intellectual giants like Tiro ... Willis ... should lack an international faculty to bestow fellowships carrying international recognition and value." Sims recommended, therefore, that in future the shorthand world congresses should bestow the title of doctor. The Encyclopaedia Britannica, that great work of reference, said in its yearbook for the congress year 1937 that the world needs a simple shorthand system easily learnable for general purposes. Had at that time the Stolze-Schrey system been suitably explained to the world congress (it was not represented), the Encyclopaedia Britannica could have indicated a solution.

I believe that when writing this little book in 1955 I was the first to coin the following two terms and to consider them essential for the formation of an ideal shorthand system:

1. the duration of pronunciation of a sound, and
2. the musical aspect of recording speech.

To these should be added the inherited tendencies

facilitating the derivation of shorthand from longhand and from word pictures preceding the latter, as also the inadequately considered association of ideas whereby each shorthand sign should contain one or more of the characteristics of the corresponding longhand sign. Of all systems, that of Stolze-Schrey has taken most of these points into account so that in this system the investigation of word and letter frequencies in all languages can be restricted to choosing word-signs for the most-used words, as is already done in longhand and print. Therefore, at the next shorthand world congress the two terms "duration of pronunciation" and "the musical aspect of recording speech" should be illustrated and recommended for consideration.

I hope that this little book will help to explain much which, though essential for a better understanding of shorthand generally, is not yet widely known. Everyone who has much writing to do should learn shorthand. Writing and reading foreign adaptations of a shorthand system facilitate learning a foreign language. When writing shorthand it is advisable to write lightly and hold the pencil at right angles to the paper with the fingers well bent.

Bibliography

Jaume Boada—in Catalan (Imprenta Nacional, Montevideo. 1955)—kindly presented to me by the author, D. Dalmau, Director of Belpost-Tecnopost, Barcelona.

Franz Xaver Gabelsberger—in German by Dr. A. Mentz (Hackners Verlag, Wolfenbuettel. 1948).

Francisco de Páula Martí Mora—in Spanish by Ventura Pascual y Beltran and Concepcion Porcel (Libreria Hernando S.A., Madrid. 1943)—kindly presented to me by J. Rius, President of the Academia de Taquigrafía, Barcelona.

Stenografiens Historia—in Swedish by Olof Werling Melin (Nordiska Bokhandeln, Stockholm. 1927).

The Story of British Shorthand—in English by E. H. Butler (Sir Isaac Pitman & Son, Ltd., London. 1951).

The biography, referred to above, of the highly-gifted Martí (born 1761 at San Felipe de Játiva, Spain; died 1827, Lisbon) describes also his work as an artist and as inventor of the fountain pen (the latter before 1802). Famous older histories of shorthand are largely out of print. Textbooks of individual shorthand systems sometimes also contain interesting historical details.